Consider this...

(About commonsense, God and Jesus Christ)

Prem Boaz

(Cover by ninabojovic.hotmail.com)

Forward

In today's market place of religious thought and products it can be difficult to sort through all of the superficial doctrines to find a compelling argument for a sound Christian faith. Many of the expressions of Christianity that claim to be "Biblically Based" are often just one person's or one group's select reading of the Biblical narrative. If you do not accept their literal interpretations of God's Divine powers without question, you are labeled as either ignorant or a heretic. Six day of creation means, "Six twenty four hour periods", and yes all the animals we know to exist where on the ark!

What has been missing from this the discussion of Christian faith is a rational approach to theology that seeks to find common ground within the Christian story for a thoughtful conversation with sound academic and scientific reasoning.

Prem Boaz in his book, Consider this. . . (About commonsense, God and Jesus), is able to merge his professional logic with the depth of his thoughtfulness and faith. In so doing, he has spelled out for us a convincing case for the "theist" view of God. Yes, faith can be defined as "the acceptance of things not seen," it can also be defined as "the commonsense outcome of a quest for knowledge and understanding."

How do Biblical narratives and the rich history of the Christian faith speak to the modern mind and soul? These are questions whose full answers still elude us, but in the search for those answers we can find meaning and purpose in the story of God's love for all humanity. Instead of ignoring the hard questions, Prem addresses the very difficult issues: What happens when we die? Is there a God? Why does he allow natural calamity? Why is there evil in the world? And finally the big question, "Does it matter if we prefer not to recognize God?"

In his concluding chapter, "Jesus Christ" we are challenged to think about the meaning of the divine- human relationship. Are we simply individual creations who are meant to live in isolation or are we all imbued with a yearning to connect with God and with each other; and if so how are we able to connect with a divine creator?

Consider this...offers a logical conclusion that the expression of God's love in Jesus Christ is how that relationship can be made.

While Prem does not purport to speak for all Christians or people of faith, he does speak for those who are willing to think long and hard about the deep questions of life.

I commend the reading of this manuscript to those whose search has led them to believe in a personal God of love and grace; and to those who are still trying to come to terms with their own scientific understanding and their acceptance of this very same God. While you may not agree with all of his conclusions, you will find it difficult to fault his logic and reasoning.

Thank you Prem, for a refreshing look at the Christian faith through the heart and mind of a scientist.

Pastor Dr. Calvin Gittner, Rev. DMin
Major. US Air force (Retired)
Port Orange Presbyterian Church
Port Orange, Fl. USA

Preface

I have always felt that Christianity is not a religion based on "blind faith" but on sound logic. Saroja, my wife, asked me if I would be willing to write to our children describing my concept of God and my reason for being a Christian. So the following started as a letter to my children.

Having been an engineer by profession, my reports and presentations during my career had been based on hard numbers, and proven laws of physics, chemistry, and material properties. So, I was a little skeptical as to how convincing my letter was going to turn out since the nature of this subject is not conducive to numerical analysis.

I realized that before I could even start on my concept of God, I first had to delve into the nature of man. Specifically, I needed to understand the difference between man as an animal and man as a person. I soon realized that one would need blind faith in the evolution theory to accept human beings as creatures evolved wholly from the elements in the world. Further, to shun God, one would have to ignore any natural curiosity as to where even the elements came from. With this realization I was able to proceed with this letter, which turned out to be too long for a letter. So my letter has become a booklet.

This booklet became possible because Saroja put in her efforts in proof reading and getting me back on the track when my thoughts occasionally wandered off in a tangent.

I dedicate this book to my wife and my five children,

Prem Boaz

Chapter 1

Commonsense

When I was very young and my parents were "all in all" in my life, whatever they said was taken by me as full truth. In fact I did not even know the difference between truth and fiction. It is at this stage we are said to "think like a child". Our confidence in our parents and what they tell us begins to form the foundation of our basic character, and many beliefs. If our parents went to Church every Sunday, we naturally went along with them as one of their extensions. It was of course "the thing to do".

One of the earliest teachings of my parents and my Sunday school teachers was that man was created by God "in His image". To a child this meant "to look just like Him". I saw paintings on the wall showing an old man with a white beard touching the hand of a younger man with a scared look, as in the famous painting of Michael Angelo in his depiction of God giving life to man. It was implied that this painting was a real depiction of what happened. Thinking like a child I took it all in. I saw a picture of a man with a long white beard knocking at a front door. I was told that it was God trying to get in. Thinking like a child, I wanted to open the door so He could come in. Whenever there was a cloud shading the sun and the rays of the sun shone around the cloud, I was told it was God standing behind the cloud. Thinking like a child I watched it in awe.

I was told that this God whom I pictured in my nascent mind, created everything seen and un-seen. As a result I pictured an old man, a humanoid, with a long and grey beard, holding a staff and walking among the stars in space, rolling up the stars and planets in his palm and releasing them into space. When I thought and reasoned like a child I took everything I heard from older people literally.

As I began to learn about space and stars and planets I realized that it is impossible for God, the old man, to be wandering around in outer space. The assumed truths began to start shaking at the foundation. I was intelligent enough to rely on what I could see, touch and feel to create my world based on the knowledge I had gained.

At this stage in life I began to question the knowledge and beliefs of my parents and other elders in my circle. I did, however, decide to tolerate their apparent "ignorance" out of respect for them. In my mind, the issue of God was put to rest. I thought that I knew what my parents believed and I politely disagreed in my head.

As I grew older, I was exposed to several distinctly different types of knowledge bases. I was truly growing wiser by the day. For example, scientific data on physics, chemistry, and mathematics belonged to one category. Another was the psychology of human behavior and interaction between people. A vastly diverse and large field of intellectual challenges and curiosity occupied most of my time, and the old subject of "God" was pretty much forgotten.

Somewhere along the continuum of my life several questions began to dawn in my mind. They began as a dull flicker of light and slowly grew in intensity and turned into a continuous flood light that I was not able to ignore. I began to wonder who we are and how we got here. I even wondered how and why the world got here – even the Big Bang theory did not explain why it happened.

Science has tried, and to a large extent succeeded, in explaining the physical development of the body of living organisms, through the process of evolution. However, there are some gaps in this explanation when it is applied to humans. The process of natural selection explains very well how certain physical traits of the living organism develop in such a way that this development helps that specific organism to survive longer within its environment. This longevity helps to reproduce more and thus, over several generations, that trait becomes an assigned attribute. In this field we are able to explain how things work. However, any attempt at explaining life in terms of the various molecular components in a living cell of the collective body, leaves something blank and wanting. The absence of an external force orchestrating the various elements to converge at the right proportion and at the right sequence and over a right period, can only result in a lifeless mixture of elements. Mere statistical probability does not explain the origin of life. Even a basic question why a living organism wants to replicate seems to be a mystery. While science, as expected, is getting better over time at explaining the evolution phenomenon, scientists are still not able to explain what "life" is. It is simply outside the reach of physical science.

The next level of complexity comes when we explore the human intelligence. We are able to study and marvel at the intelligence levels of various primates and other animals such as dolphins and elephants. But there is no scale big enough to compare them even remotely with the intelligence of humans. There is one plausible explanation for this huge difference. One definition of intelligence is the ability to use available information. Since information leads to more information, this bank of data, feeding on itself, is in a constant state of enrichment. Thus the human intelligence which is dependent on this data moves forward as well, creating specialists and super specialists in their chosen fields of interest. While this phenomenon might explain what happened to us humans it does not explain why this process did not happen to any of the other creatures. It is of interest to note that even the chimpanzees, our closest primates up the scale of evolution, are still around sporting chimpanzee brains. Again this seems to suggest some external interest in our extraordinary gift of creative intelligence.

There are some glaring limitations in our ability to perceive or explain certain barriers to our intelligence. The concept of infinity such as the expanse of astronomical open space is one such item. However hard we try we are not able to grasp what is beyond space. We seem to run into a virtual hard shell. It is like we live inside a hollow steel ball where we have morphed from nothing and we are trying to explain what might be outside the wall. We have to swallow our pride and accept our Limited Brain Capacity - LBC.

Recognizing our LBC, we now face some very intriguing facts about us humans. Some of these facts are beyond the simple explanation of the mechanical process of evolution. The explanations for the various feelings we have such as, love, hate, compassion, admiration, fairness, etc., do not readily fit into the time scale of the physical evolution model. Some psychologists have concluded that even the inherent attributes of love and grace are evolved natures as man learned to interact with others in communities. Archeological evidence shows that humans started to live in small communities such as Harappa and Mohenjo - Daro only about five thousand years ago. Even the Stone Age settlements take us back to only about 10,000 years. Prior to that the bands of humans most probably ,only consisted of not more than a male and his dependents, such as his mates and off springs, very similar to the groups of animals we see even today. Ancient narrations such as the Vedas, about 5000 years ago, are already referring to man's grace of forgiving the enemy. The established time scale of evolution process does not allow for the adaptation of fairness, love, and grace in such a short time, without an external encouragement. There is clearly another force at play that defines us and separates us from other forms of life. This is a fact that we have to accept. Logic and commonsense do not allow any other alternative.

The influence of this extraordinary force on us humans has been the subject of wonder and discussion among scholars for thousands of years. We see evidence of this discussion within the Old Testament of the Bible as well as other several old writings around the world. The early books within the Bible were written about three thousand years ago. The style of presenting an idea in writing changes in as little as a few hundred years. Thus, reading three thousand year old writings presents a problem on how to decipher the intent of the author. To understand what the author was saying, the reader has to allow for the norm that existed three thousand years ago on how observations and thoughts were recorded. Added to that is the smaller base of human knowledge on natural forces at that time. We cannot simply read an Old Testament book like a modern novel written yesterday. For example a bolt of lightning was not a discharge of electron from the clouds. It was more like a pillar of fire. The thunder was not the propagation of electron beam breaking the sound barrier, but an expression of anger from an unknown source. Even the fire was not a rapid oxidation of an organic matter, but the consumption of evil by a superior force. Any natural phenomenon that caused destruction elicited great fear and sometimes the authors of the old scriptures also seemed to indulge in much exaggeration to make a point.

One basic perception comes through clearly in the Old Testament as well as other ancient writings. The authors were very much aware of the force that influenced human behavior. They referred to this force as God. To them, God was to be feared as they saw all natural disasters as acts of God or as punishment from God. Several centuries later when we became more knowledgeable of natural forces this fear appears to have been diminished.

The authors of the Gospels in the New Testament make it very clear that the advent and life of Jesus of Nazareth fully changed the concept of fear of God to the love and grace of God. Such a significant, fundamental change in the basic tenet of a religious faith is not seen in any other religious scripture but in the Bible. Adaptation of this transition is unique to Christianity.

Here then, in summary, are some of the facts we face:

1. Our LBC is real and we simply cannot explain everything around us.
2. While the evolution theory explains the physical development of plants and animals it does not explain much beyond. The origin of life and the "emotions" humans experience are some of them.

3 There is clearly a force that is responsible for the creation of life and the complex nature of the human mind.

4 Many would like to define this force that also guides us towards grace and fairness, as God.

In our busy life as adults, we may not allocate much time to ponder these issues. However, consciously or unconsciously, we do subscribe to one of the following two choices.

Choice1: Simply dis-regard these observations as irrelevant and do not accept the existence of God.

This choice may not harm a person. If you worked hard you can get ahead on personal strength alone. Your conscience will continue to encourage you to support worthwhile charitable efforts and to do many good deeds. There is a reason why you want to do good things. You may not want to accept this, but God is already working from within. He has implanted a conscience.

Choice2: Accept the presence of this force, this God, as real and recognize the fact that one is never alone.

This choice starts with you recognizing yourself as the bearer of God's influence within you. You may never understand how God works. But, in everything you do you are no longer alone. You have a built in Friend working with you. You will know that your life has more meaning.

It is just plain commonsense as to which choice is more advantageous.

Chapter 2

The issue of God

An atheist was once asked to describe or define that part of the concept of God in which he does not believe. He said that it was not possible for him to do so as he was being asked to define something that, in his opinion, does not exist. Therefore, it is a theistic burden to define God.

 Atheists appear to be quite convinced that all aspects of human character - physical, emotional, intellectual, creativity, etc., are the result of natural physical and psychological evolution. Man's very existence is a mere statistical event resulting from the interaction within a vast pool of chemical elements and natural events. If that was indeed the case, the atheists want to know, where the question of God comes in. "We are born, we live, we die, end of the story". On the other hand a theist believes that there is more to "life". The theist believes that man is an embodiment of a level of intelligence, emotions and a capacity for grace and fairness that is outside the realm of statistical events followed by psychological evolution and that an external influence, God, is involved. This is the main difference between atheism and theism. It comes down to the issue of how we reconcile with the role that God plays in human life.

Modern scientists are able to postulate that life on this earth must have started some 4 billion years ago. It is not possible to explain why it happened. The mere issue of how it happened is complex enough. According to them, even at the smallest bacterial level, the formation of the first cell required a very large number of specific organic molecules to be present and assembled in a specific order. The statistical probability of this event, if it occurred by chance, is extremely low due to the vast number of molecules and the specific order of assembly involved. Even if it did happen once by chance, the probability of it happening repeatedly is akin to the possibility of the same lucky set of numbers showing up over and over again in a mega lottery draw. If it did happen in a lottery draw, it will be proper to attribute the events to some external manipulation of the process and not to a mere statistical possibility. In addition, the first living cells had to survive the extremely harsh environment present four billion years ago, which they did. There had to have been a force to overcome the statistical improbability of the multiple cell formation, to overcome the harsh environment, and to give reason to replicate etc. Theists call this force God. It is not logistic, but "blind faith", to accept that all these happened by "chance".

Both theists and atheists agree that several aspects of our world and our lives are beyond our comprehension due to our limited brain capacity (LBC). For example, when we try to comprehend the universe, the concept of "nothing" and then from this nothing large numbers – in billions – of stars moving away is one such phenomenon. Atheists are content to simply ignore this mystery or pretend that merely giving this a name "big bang" is adequate. Theists ask who or what power or force put these galaxies in motion and from where? And who gave us the senses to be able perceive them the way we do? Theists prefer to refer to this force, as coming from "God". While this defines God as the creator of the universe, their definition of God goes beyond this in a more personal level. For example, there are many aspects of human behavior that cannot be attributed to mere natural evolution required for survival. There clearly is a guiding force involved.

Does Man comply with the evolution theory one hundred percent?

It is proven that over time, nature seems to fine tune the physique to suit the environment. However, certain human behaviors such as appreciation of abstract art, good conscience, grace, the desire to be fair, etc., cannot be explained with this simple evolution theory.

Consider, our appreciation of communication through arts and music. If this trait is strictly a development that is a result of a social setting, and a result from a need to improve efficient communication of one's inner thoughts and ideas, as may be explained by the evolution process, then the origin of this development must coincide with the period when man started to live in communities. All recorded anthropological evidence show that man started to live in small communities about nine to ten thousand years ago. That being the case, to what motivation can we assign the fact that man indulged in creating graceful arts, some forty thousand years ago such as the ones found in Cantabria, Spain? It will seem that forty thousand years ago the isolated man's main concern would have been to run from predators, kill or forage for food and find a safe place to sleep. Wanting to create a work of art would have been an extraordinary effort motivated by his inherent creative talent and a desire for self-expression. It will appear that this creative talent was, and is, part of man's possession of a 'soul' and not merely a mechanical, physical, and development process to facilitate survival.

About five thousand years ago we learned to record information and our thoughts in a media for preservation. One would expect that when humans were first able to write in prose, the bulk of their work would involve mainly items such as , for example, "how to skin a buffalo with the ragged edge of a rock" or, something along that line needed for his survival and wellbeing. However we find that some of the earliest writings involve exploration of right and wrong of human behavior and possible controlling forces of their behavior. They were already referring to these forces and other philosophical thoughts as gods. Since then we became creatures with extraordinary capabilities in our cognitive and creative capacity. We developed a whole slew of characters that apply solely to humans.

From an atheistic point of view, the human evolution is no more miraculous than that of the evolution of the fruit fly.

Can we "not have" a Soul?

We developed a sense of "self" – a highly personal concept of who we are and what our values are. This is simply the human nature. When we try to look into our inner self we find that we are filled with feelings of right and wrong, moral and immoral, love and hate etc. The list of feelings can be very long. There is one word that refers to this unique concept of 'self'. It is what we call our "Soul". Without this soul within us, we are merely a machine, run by a super computer, a well-engineered humanoid organic machine.

This soul of a person seems to be present from the time of birth. Very young children are able to display the presence of their soul in their smile even before they have learned to talk. Also, an innate conscience of right and wrong is present in early childhood as this real life story shows.

A four year old child was traveling with his parents on a sightseeing tour. One of their stops was at a small handicraft plant where they were producing natural silk threads. Silk worms form cocoons by wrapping their bodies with thin threads of silk produced from their saliva. The worms are protected from the environment and predators by this silk cocoon shell until they are ready to come out as mature silk moths. To extract the silk threads the silk crafts men collect the cocoons by the hundreds and boil them in water to loosen the threads. They then collect the silk threads with a brush like tool and send the threads for further processing. After this demonstration the parents of this child noticed that he was very sad and withdrawn. Being attentive parents they immediately knew that something was really bothering this child. On talking to him they realized that the killing of all those silk worms within the cocoon was terribly upsetting to this child. His conscience was bothering him. His little heart was breaking.

God defined as the source of our Soul.

Theists believe that the source of our souls is "God". Due to evolution, many animals developed physical traits as well as behavioral instincts for survival. However, the embodiment of a soul in humans presents an image that is immensely more complex than any other life forms that has evolved through the same four billion years. There obviously is a force that has caused a soul to be an innate part of the human. Theists believe that to deny this God, one has to describe himself as a person without a soul and that will be a blatant denial of obvious truth.

Some issues with acceptance of "God".

Among many of the younger generation, the mere use of the word "God" raises a resistance to conceptual acceptance.

They would like to see some questions answered.

1. Is there proof that there is God?

2. Why should I allow some mythical "king of kings" or any such royal character to replace my own good conscience?
3. Can the existence of God explain what happens when we die?
4. If there is a God, why does he allow natural calamity where we live?
5. If there is God, why does He allow evil actions by humans?

These questions require thoughtful consideration.

The demand for proof

People want tangible and perceptible proof before they can accept the existence of God. It is a disappointing fact that the existence of God can never be proven any more clearly than we can prove that the "mind' exists. The fact that our thoughts lead to actions, is evidence that our minds exist. The solution rests on how we define "God". If we define God as the nucleus of the force that is behind our good conscience, our creative mind and our soul, then, under this definition, the existence of God becomes evident.

Consider this: Our senses allow us to see, touch, feel, measure and comprehend a whole lot of elements, and their combinations amounting to objects as small as an atom to as big as the earth, Stars etc. We know that they exist. Concerning their existence the theist has one of two things to say. 1. "God made all these things" or 2. "These things are here and I wish to define whoever made these as "God". Once again, in either case, the existence of God is self-evident.

Is God a lofty character?

The mere thought of God as an external controlling force that some refer to as "King of Kings", "Lord supreme", "Almighty", "up on the golden throne" etc. simply turns many off. Those terminologies were the norm of expression in the early centuries when Kings and lords were indeed a big deal. In our modern times the very concept of Royalty seems to have lost much respect, except perhaps in Britain. There the people love their Royalties not out of fear and awe but because they love the tradition and civility they project. God is not royalty. In fact He is not even a person. To the theists, God is more accessible, much closer, dearer and more personal than any king or potentate has ever been or will be in human history.

What happens when we die?

One common reason many reject the existence of God is their disappointment that the concept of God does not provide clear answers on what happens to a person after death. The various descriptions by religious writers on this subject, to them, are merely opinions and recollection of dreams with no proof. An atheistic view, at least provides a simple assurance that everything ends with the death of the body.

Consider this: Moderns science has established that the human body, after it took millions of years to evolve to its current level of sophistication, has a theoretical maximum of 120 years to function. It is preprogrammed to self-destruct within this assigned time. While the body feels the weight of time, and becomes feeble with age, the soul that occupies the body is immune to the time scale. The existence of this body seems to be merely a flash in the total scheme of life on earth. But, the soul, since it not an organic physical entity, does not age. For a theist the question is "what happens to the soul when it's time with the physical body expires?" When the soul resides within the body, the human is endowed with a spiritual world around him as defined by his soul. The theist believes that this spiritual world continues to exist after death as it is not a "time" related function as we perceive time.

It is a moving experience to feel the soul of a person when he or she dies. How strongly we feel their soul is a function of how emotionally close we were when that person was alive. It does not depend on the physical age of the deceased. It is as though the soul has very little to do with the age of the body.

This is the main difference between atheistic and theistic view of death. For an atheist the physical body is the only point of focus. It is the beginning and end, a mere collection of chemical elements going back to their original state. For a theist the body does end but the soul continues in a spiritual world.

Why does God allow natural calamity?

Prior to addressing the issue of natural calamities we need to remember that natural phenomenon such as ice age, volcanoes, fire, earthquakes, hurricanes, mass flooding etc. were some of the environmental challenges we faced as the human body was still evolving to survive these challenges. It will appear that without evolutionary adaptation, and God's gifts such as creative talents we would have been an extinct species along with many that are indeed extinct. We have been dealing with natural disasters for a very long time. Zoological scientists have determined that many animals are continuing to become extinct due to natural changes in their habitat.

One of the major gifts that we have as humans that other animals do not have is this: We have a creative ability that allows us to shape the environment that we choose to live in. While birds and certain animals are able to build nests and Burroughs for a place to sleep in and raise their offspring, man is able to map out hazardous regions such as geological fault lines and flood zones before he decides where he wants to live.

This world has some 58 million square miles of land within which we choose where we want to live.

When we live in an area that is known to carry the risk of hurricanes and earth quakes etc., it is because that happens to be our choice. When disasters do strike in the form of unexpected deluge of rain, or prolonged drought, or tsunami, etc. we find that we have been given the inner strength, and love and support from other humans to cope with it. We find that such disasters induce stronger bonds between humans. Besides, if God were to eliminate such major calamities, what we now consider as minor calamities will then stand out as major. Thus if God were to continue to eliminate the latest list of major calamities, there can be no end. Theoretically, every challenge we have in life will have to go away leaving humans as a mere blob of life with nothing to do. In other words, God has to draw the line somewhere or loose the identity of his prized creation.

Why does God allow evil actions by people against another?

Very few people go through their life wanting to be "evil". It is not natural that we have an entry in our calendar that says, "Today I am going to be an evil person". We find that even when a person does something evil, he generally tries to justify it as having done it for a "good' cause. History shows that evil and good rule our soul ranging from, the examples of Hitler to mother Theresa. Our actions are a result of our freewill. If God wants to forcibly stop men from making evil choices, He will have to take away the freewill and that will take away our will to be good as well. This will turn him into a mere humanoid body with no soul – just a puppet.

The big question

The big question is, while there is the influence of God within us whereby we know right from wrong, good from bad, does it make a difference if we prefer not to recognize this God?

Many go through life not recognizing God, but live good lives. Their life is guided by their good conscience. The reality is that whether we realize it or not, God is already at work influencing our mind and conscience.

Unfortunately, while there is a force encouraging us to do everything that is good, that we call God, there is also another force trying to guide us through a deviant path. Some people refer to this force as the "evil force" or Satan. This force has a way of sneaking into our mind. It often succeeds in making us do things which our normal conscience does not condone.

When we refuse to recognize God, we are inadvertently dealing the evil force a winning hand. Our refusal to recognize God, creates an opening in our soul and that gives evil a clear shot at our minds. We become more vulnerable. It appears that about 2000 years ago, the evil almost got the upper hand.

Something very significant happened some 2000 years ago.

When we conclude that it was God, as defined and recognized by us, who created the basic elements that make the world, or that God gave us the very senses that perceive the vastness of the galaxy, or that it is this God's will that we are endowed with a good conscious, or that our soul is guided by God, or that our creative mind is a gift from God, we are indeed reaching for the limits of the space within our LBC. To come to these conclusions, we can only use our resources within this limited shell. Even the intellectual giants of the past and present are forced to work within this shell. Two thousand years ago it would appear that we had a break through. It was not a result of our effort, but our transgressions. We had a visitor from outside the shell of our LBC. This visitor was clearly so much outside our LBC to the point that the religious people and the governing authorities nailed Him to a cross. But, within a period of just two years, He was able to portray to us the vision of the kingdom of God. He came to us as a human so He can relate to us at the human level. It is recorded that He "wept" like a human and later during His trial for His life, the Roman army officer asked Him "do you not realize that I have the power to release you?" Jesus replied, "You have no power over me other than what my Father gives you". This was an answer no man would have dared to give to a Roman officer. Clearly He was God and human all at once.

The advent of this Jesus changed the course of the history of man.

Chapter 3

Jesus Christ

About Jesus Christ, Dr. James Allan Francis (1864 - 1928), said this:

"….When we try to sum up his influence, all the armies that ever marched, all the parliaments that ever sat, all the kings that ever reigned are absolutely picayune (insignificant) in their influence on mankind compared with that of this one solitary life…". (The full script as written by Dr. James Allan Francis in its original form is added at the end of this chapter)

What is interesting is that he was merely stating a historical fact.

 The only other event that may come close, in its influence on the direction of flow of human history, is perhaps when the "greatest generation" of American men and women, volunteered to rid the menace Hitler of Europe. That cost about 400,000 American lives and it was a six year effort. Jesus preached for a mere two years before he was executed. Today about one third of the world's population identify themselves as followers of the teachings of Jesus.

Clearly there was something unique about this man, Jesus of Nazareth. He had a clear mission. That mission was to persuade people not to follow an evil path but to turn around in their own cognizance. In doing so he wanted man to obtain a clear vision of a world completely under the influence of the good force, the same force that induces a natural tendency in man to shun evil. In other words he wanted man to open his eyes and see what He referred to as the "kingdom of God".

I would like to present at least four facets of Jesus Christ that require our thoughtful consideration.

1. Was there really a man called Jesus of Nazareth some 2000 years ago, who preached for two years and then was executed on a cross by the Roman authorities at the urging of the Jewish priests?
2. If this Jesus did exist, and he preached, what was his message?

3. Is the 2000 years old message from Jesus have any credence in today's world?
4. Was this Jesus truly an extension of God?

Was there really a man called Jesus?

Fortunately, 2000 years old historical event falls well within the verifiable archeological age. These events are fully recorded and authenticated by hard evidence. We know with some certainty the place and the year when Jesus was born, as well as the political and religious atmosphere that existed at that time. We also know the details of his trial and his execution on the cross. Execution by being nailed to a cross was the common mode of capital punishment in those days. It was metered out to common criminals and political and religious renegades.

What was the message that was preached by this Jesus?

Most People including many atheists agree that the messages delivered by Jesus were, and still are, meaningful after 2000 years. We find His messages to be absolutely profound. This includes

people who do not identify themselves as
Christians.

- He taught simple but powerful ideas such as "treat others as you will want others to treat you".
- He wanted us to love our enemies. As He put it, ".... love your enemies, and pray for those who persecute you in order that you may be sons of your Father who is in heaven; for He causes His sun to rise on the evil and the good, and sends rain on the righteous and the unrighteous. For if you love those who love you, what reward have you? Do not even the tax-gatherers do the same?"
- Jesus wanted us to be watchful not to judge others of wrong doing, as it is possible that we are not worthy of that task having indulged in wrong doings ourselves.
- He wanted us to resist our anger. Psychologists are able to show how pent up anger deteriorates our health from the inside. As Jesus explained it, even if we are in the midst of offering a gift at the altar, If we remembered that we are angry with our brother, we should leave the gift before the

alter and go make peace with our brother first.

- Giving alms to the poor is emphasized by Jesus several times. However, He made it very clear that whatever we give, needs to be kept a secret as it is really between us and God. Similarly, when we pray to God, he wanted us to keep it private as it is a private matter between us and God.   He even taught us how to pray. The Bible has recorded this format for prayer as the Lord's Prayer.
- Jesus made it very clear that following His commandments is like building our house on a foundation of rock. Conversely, not following his commandments is like building a house on sand. He summarized His commandments as follows.

1. "Thou shalt love the Lord thy God with thy whole heart, and with thy whole soul, and with thy whole mind, and with thy whole strength".
2. "Thou shalt love thy neighbor as thyself."

How pertinent is Jesus's 2000 year old message in today's world?

Consider this message from Jesus that man should reach for the kingdom of God by forgiving his enemies. He gave this message literally with His last dying breath. Jesus said on the cross "Father forgive them for they know not what they do".

If we study the ongoing killings between different factions in the Middle East and elsewhere in the world we find that practically in every incident the factions that took the blame/credit for the killing insist that they did it in revenge for an earlier incident where they were the victims. This endless chain of killings can only be broken when Christ's message of forgiving your enemy takes hold. Only by breaking one link, by one faction deciding to forgive, will this toxic chain of events cease.

Consider this sad truth: There are some communities in today's world where people, adults, children, and infants live in dwellings on top of decaying garbage piles. Here they compete with rodents for any scrap of food that may be found on this pile. They find shelter from rain with card board boxes or rusted sheet metals over their head for a roof. The lucky ones who manage to get away from these dwellings are allowed to huddle against the gutter side of tall buildings. Even the most creative artists who were able to depict "hell" with flames and hot flowing lava and creatures with tails and sharp spears standing guard, cannot create such a terrible place for the destitute. It is as though Satan has managed to establish his version of hell before Jesus's kingdom of God is allowed to take root. These ghettos merely represent the difference between the "haves" and the "have-nots" in today's world community. One possible way to end this living hell will be when the haves decide to follow Jesus's request "If you love me feed my lamb".

Consider this city bustling with activities and people hurrying about attending to their business. You see a man or a woman in tattered clothes obviously starving and walking in a daze, perhaps even aware that he or she is dying from some terminal illness, and the rest of the people walk around this person without the slightest sign of recognizing their plight. In many parts of the world this city does exist. To this man or woman, hell does exist and they are in it. Here is an opportunity for the others to reach for the kingdom of God. Jesus said this very plainly when He said, "Love thy neighbor".

 We do find that in every situation in life, an opportunity exists for applying one of Jesus's teachings. What Jesus preached some 2000 years ago is indeed relevant today.

Was Jesus Christ truly an extension of God?

Christians believe that God decided to come to man as a man, and that man was Jesus the Christ, the Messiah. However, the very concept of God coming among men as a man is simply too difficult for many to accept or to even comprehend.

The problem with accepting Jesus as an extension of God seems to come from one's very concept of God Himself. If one's concept of God is a mythical figure such as an artistic creation, then along with this myth the advent of Jesus also disappears. If on the other hand, if one is able to see God as the natural force that wants human to be "good" and shun "evil", then it is very logical that this force, this God, will want to come to this world as a man himself and give His message on how to live in this world.

Looking back through man's religious quest on finding God we realize that there are hundreds of holy, God fearing men, both mythical and real, who had great influence on humanity. Their teachings have been profound. If men were to follow their instructions they will truly find themselves getting closer to God. They teach us how not to stray from the path that leads to God. Their teachings lead men in a journey that is never ending. Here is the significant difference between Jesus and all the other holy, real life, men in history.

When we accept Jesus as God, we accept God coming into this world as man and our journey to find Him is over. This is a claim that only Jesus is able make.

Consider this: After a mere two years of evangelizing, Jesus was killed on a cross. His close knit followers were terrified as they witnessed what was happening to their master/teacher. They knew that they would be identified as followers of Jesus. They knew that they were facing the same fate at the hands of the same Jewish and other authorities who felt threatened by this new concept of "kingdom of God". Under normal conditions Jesus's followers would have scattered and gone into hiding and that would have been the end of the story of Jesus. Jesus would have been recorded in the history books as another holy and good man who ran afoul with the then religious authorities, and nothing more.

Now consider this: Several independent first hand reports claim the sighting of Jesus among the disciples, soon after the crucifixion. Directly from Jesus, the disciples received the courage, the command and the charter to go and spread His message among all the people in the world. This explains why the disciples of Jesus did not run and hide. History records that eleven of the twelve disciple's lives ended in violent death. But, not before Jesus's words take root. Within a few years after Jesus's death, the number of believers in his teachings as the way to the kingdom of God, increased exponentially.

Clearly, this man Jesus was more than just another holy man.

Man's attempt to reach God

Going back to ancient days and even today, humans have always tried to reach God. They might take a journey of several thousand miles fraught with danger and discomfort, to reach a spot that they believe to be closer to God. They might make sacrifices of wealth and personal comfort as gestures to please and get closer to God. People of all religions in the world embark on these journeys called pilgrimages.

For example, there are certain hills in India where a Hindu temple is built at the highest point, as close as possible to reach the heaven above. Holy, god fearing men climb the hillside carrying a humble gift for god to be laid inside the temple. However, these man do not want to desecrate the path to god by trampling the way with their feet. To climb the hill, they roll up the hill keeping their feet and the gift from touching the ground. The result is that, by the time they reach the top, their body is full of bleeding scuff marks and scratches. Their desire to reach god is so strong that they do not mind the severe damage to their body. This is just one example of man's unquenchable desire to unite with god. Throughout the world and throughout all the religious beliefs and practices we find this one common passion – the need to reach one's god.

<u>God's attempt to reach man</u>

Consider this: The most celebrated and significant feature of God coming to be among man as a man himself is that God negated the need for man to struggle to reach God. Christians believe that In Christ, God has come down, reached man, and taught us how to love God and love one another.

One Solitary life

(The original version by Dr. James Allan Francis)

"Let us turn now to the story. A child is born in an obscure village. He is brought up in another obscure village. He works in a carpenter shop until he is thirty, and then for three brief years is an itinerant preacher, proclaiming a message and living a life. He never writes a book. He never holds an office. He never raises an army. He never has a family of his own. He never owns a home. He never goes to college. He never travels two hundred miles from the place where he was born. He gathers a little group of friends about him and teaches them his way of life. While

*still a young man, the tide of popular feeling
turns against him. One denies him; another
betrays him. He is turned over to his enemies.
He goes through the mockery of a trial; he is
nailed to a cross between two thieves, and
when dead is laid in a borrowed grave by the
kindness of a friend.*

*Those are the facts of his human life. He rises
from the dead. Today we look back across
nineteen hundred years and ask, what kind of
trail has he left across the centuries? When
we try to sum up his influence, all the armies
that ever marched, all the parliaments that
ever sat, all the kings that ever reigned are
absolutely picayune in their influence on
mankind compared with that of this one
solitary life"…*

6207618R00028

Made in the USA
San Bernardino, CA
03 December 2013